Outdoor Science Adventures

by MELVIN BERGER
Illustrated by G. BRIAN KARAS

SCHOLASTIC INC.

New York Toronto London Auckland Sydney

ISBN 0-590-46855-3

Text copyright © 1994 by Melvin H. and Gilda Berger Trust.
Illustrations copyright © 1994 by Scholastic Inc.
All rights reserved. Published by Scholastic Inc.

12 11 10 9 8 7 6 5 4 3 2 1   4 5 6 7 8 9/9

Printed in the U.S.A.   40

First Scholastic printing, September 1994

CONTENTS

INTRODUCTION

Would you like to
- tell time by the stars?
- start a garden?
- test for pollution?
- fly a homemade helicopter?
- identify animal tracks?
- build a birdhouse?

Outdoor Science Adventures tells you how. This book presents more than 50 science activities and experiments. You will find them easy and fun to do.

Try these adventures alone or with a friend. There are some for every season. Choose activities from the beginning, the middle, or the end of the book, depending on the weather and the time of year.

Before starting out, check the "You will need" box. You can find most of the supplies around the house. Then go outside and let your science adventures begin!

LOOK TO THE STARS

You can gaze at the stars any clear night of the year. But it's best

— just before or just after a new moon.
— when you're far from bright signs or streetlights.
— when tall buildings or trees don't block your view.

Count the Stars

No one can see all the billions of stars in the sky. But you'll be surprised at how many stars you *can* see.

> You will need: a cardboard tube from paper towels, toilet tissue, or aluminum foil.

Look up at the stars. If you can, sit down or lie on your back. Can you guess how many stars you see?

Here's how to estimate the number of stars in your sight. Look at the stars through the cardboard tube. Count the number of stars that you see through the tube.

(2 – 1500 !)

Two stars? That means you can see about 1,500 stars in the whole sky.

Three stars? That means you can see about 2,000 stars in the whole sky.

Four stars? That means you can see about 3,000 stars in the whole sky. (Probably no one has seen more than that at one time!)

Fill in:

Date: _____

No. of Stars Seen: _____

Spot the Big Dipper

Some stars form groups in the sky. The best known group is the Big Dipper. It is part of a constellation called Ursa Major, or Great Bear. It's not hard to find. And you can see it on any clear, dark night.

The Big Dipper is made up of seven bright stars. Each one has a name.

Three stars are nearly in a row. Think of a line that connects these stars. That's the handle of the dipper.

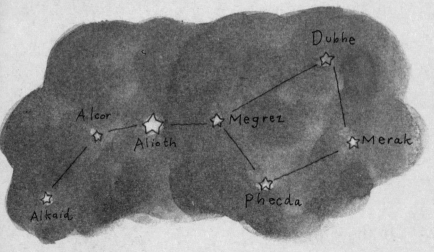

Just past the handle are four other stars. Think of a line that connects these stars. That's the cup of the dipper.

Look for the Big Dipper in the northern sky. Of course, you must face north to find it. Use a compass or a landmark to find north.

You'll always see the Big Dipper in the north. But it's not always in the exact same place.

In the winter it's
— straight north.
— low in the sky.
— with the handle pointing down.

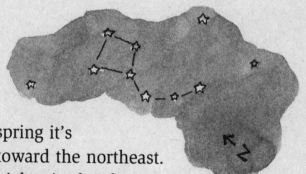

In the spring it's
— toward the northeast.
— higher in the sky.
— with the handle pointing to the side.

In the fall it's

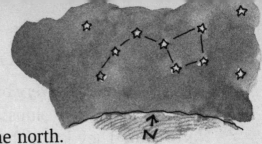

    — toward the north.
    — lower in the sky.
    — with the handle pointing to the side.

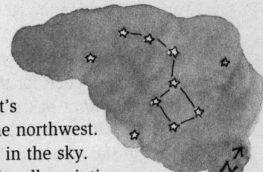

In the summer it's
    — toward the northwest.
    — very high in the sky.
    — with the handle pointing up.

Here's the date and a picture of the Big Dipper that I saw:

Date: _____

Discover the North Star

The North Star is a very bright star. Sailors used to steer their ships at night by the North Star. They knew that the North Star is always in the north. Once they found it, they could figure out all the other directions.

You can also use the North Star to figure out all the directions.

To find the North Star, you must first find the Big Dipper. Look for the two stars that make up the front of the cup. These stars are in line with another, very bright star. That bright star is the North Star, or Polaris.

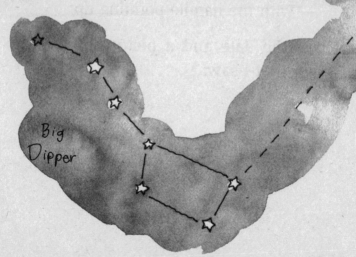

Here's how to figure out the other directions. Face north and put out your right arm.

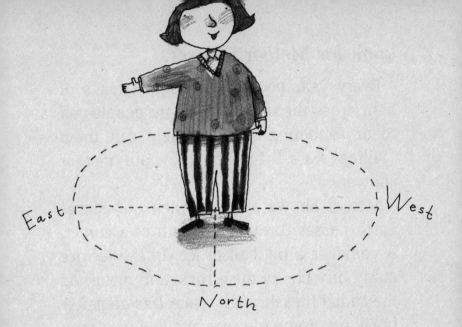

East

West

North

Turn and face that way. Now you are facing east.

Put out your right arm again and face that way. Now you are facing south.

Put out your arm one more time and face that way. Now you are facing west.

Here's a compass showing north, east, south, west:

Look for Meteor Showers

Every year people see bright streaks of light cross the night sky. Some people call them "shooting stars." Others call them "falling stars." In fact, they are meteor showers.

Meteor showers occur when our planet Earth passes through the path of a comet. A comet is a big ball of ice. In the ice are many tiny bits of dust, rock, and metal. As the comet flies through space, bits of matter break off. Some of these bits fly faster than 100,000 miles per hour! When they enter Earth's atmosphere, they are flying so fast that they get hot. They begin to shine, and they make the air glow. You see the glow as a streak of light in the sky.

The best time to see meteor showers is either very late at night or just before dawn. The shower with the brightest meteors and the most meteors comes between July 25 and August 18 every year. You may see up to 50 meteors an hour!

Here are some other bright, annual meteor showers that you can see through the year:

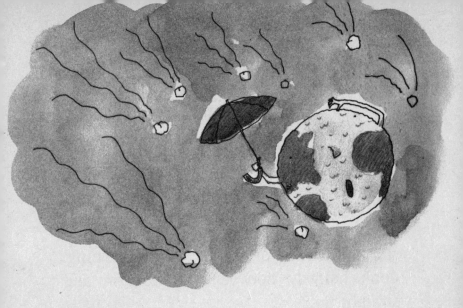

January 1–4: 50 meteors an hour.
April 19–24: 10 meteors an hour.
May 1–6: 20 meteors an hour.
October 18–23: 20 meteors an hour.
October 24–November 30: 10 meteors an hour.
December 10–13: 60 meteors an hour.

My log of meteor showers:

Date	Time	Number of Meteors

Get to Know the Stars

Certain groups of stars form pictures in the sky. They are called constellations. Orion (oh-RYE-un) is a well-known constellation. It has more bright stars than any other constellation.

Here's how to find Orion, the great hunter of Greek legend. Face southeast (between south and east) on a dark, winter evening. Look halfway between the horizon and straight up.

Find three bright stars in a row. They make up Orion's belt. The stars leading down from his belt represent a sword. The brightest star in Orion is at the tip of his right foot.

In summer and fall, you can see a band of stars. There are so many stars that they make a white path across the sky like a giant splash of milk. That's why we call this white path of stars the Milky Way.

When you are gazing at the Milky Way, you are looking toward the center of our galaxy. Our galaxy contains hundreds of billions of stars. But you can only see a few of them.

Try looking at the Milky Way through a telescope. The telescope lets you see the many separate stars that make up the Milky Way.

TEST THE AIR,
TEST THE WATER

Until about 100 years ago, the air was clean and good to breathe. Then people started building factories and driving cars. The air got very polluted in some places. How's the air where you live?

The Rubber Band Air Test

Here's a test to help you find out if the air in your community is clean or polluted. You can do it any time the temperature outside is above freezing (32°F).

> You will need: four small rubber bands, a wire clothes hanger.

Stretch the rubber bands over the hanger. Hang the hanger outdoors. Leave it there for a week.

Then look at the rubber bands. Do they look the way they did before — or are they cracked? Touch the rubber bands. Do they

feel the way they did before — or are they hard?

If they look and feel the way they did before, then the air is quite clean.

If they look cracked and feel hard, then the air is polluted.

Leave the rubber bands out for a few more weeks. The longer they don't crack or break, the cleaner the air.

Rubber Band Pollution Test

Starting Date: _____

	Looks	Feels
End of Week 1		
End of Week 2		
End of Week 3		
Conclusion:		

The Vaseline Air Test

Air pollution is not only caused by gases in the air. It is also caused by tiny bits of dust in the air. This test will help you measure the amount of dust in the air. Try to do this test when there is no rain in the forecast.

> You will need: several 3" × 5" index cards, Vaseline, tape, pencil, magnifying glass.

Spread a thin layer of Vaseline over the center of a card. Tape it, Vaseline side out, to the outside of a window in your house. If you have windows facing in different directions, make a card for each direction. If you have downstairs and upstairs windows, put some on each level. Ask a friend to do the same in his or her house.

Leave the cards up for a week. The sticky Vaseline will catch dust that flies by.

Then take the cards down. As you do,

mark the window direction (north, south, east, west) of the card.

Look closely at the Vaseline spot. A magnifying glass will help. Which cards have the most specks of dust? Which have the least? Can you figure out why?

Window	Amount of Dust
_____	_____
_____	_____
_____	_____
_____	_____

The Potato Test

Do you live near a lake, river, ocean, or other body of water? Is the water clean? Or is it polluted? This test will help you find out.

You will need: a glass bottle, a small potato, a table knife.

Collect a sample of the water. Bring it home. Ask an adult to boil one small, unpeeled potato.

Get a clean, dry, wide-mouthed glass jar. While the boiled potato is still warm, cut off one slice about ½-inch thick. Place the slice in the bottom of the jar.

Pour ¼ inch of the water sample into the jar to cover the bottom.

Put the cover on the jar. Place it in a dark, warm place. If there are germs in the water, they will grow on the potato. And germs grow best when it is dark and warm.

After a week look at the potato. Do you see fuzz on the potato? The fuzz is germs growing on the potato. You are looking at the growing germs.

Look at the potato after two weeks and three weeks. Is there fuzz on the potato? Is the amount of fuzz growing? (Look, but don't eat!)

Potato Test

Starting Date: _____

Looks

End of Week 1 _____

End of Week 2 _____

End of Week 3 _____

Conclusion: _____

UP, UP, AND AWAY!

Make a Super Loop Glider

A glider is an aircraft without a motor. It flies like a bird, on rising air currents. Here's a kind of glider you can make yourself. It's easy to do.

> You will need: a plastic straw, a piece of paper, a ruler, scissors, tape.

Cut a strip of paper about 1½ inches wide and 8½ inches long. Cut another strip 1 inch wide and 7½ inches long.

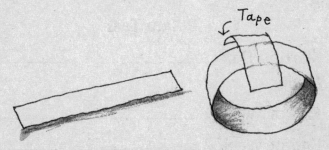

Tape

Form the strips of paper into two loops. Close the loops with small pieces of tape.

Tape the large loop to one end of the straw.
Tape the small loop to the other end.

Now you're ready to fly your glider. Toss
it into the air with the smaller loop in front.
Watch it go! Measure the distance with a
ruler.

Date: _____

Distance: _____ feet _____ inches

Fly a Helicopter

Helicopters are planes with large blades on top. The blades, or rotors, spin around. They make the helicopter fly. Here's how to make your own helicopter.

You will need: a piece of paper, a ruler, scissors, a paper clip.

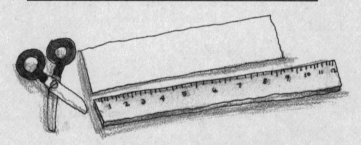

Cut a strip of paper about 2 inches wide and 9 inches long. Draw two lines that are 3 inches in from each end of the strip. Fold the two ends of the strip along the lines. This divides the strip into three equal lengths.

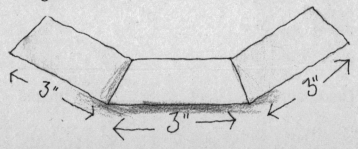

Open one fold. You are going to cut this part of the strip in half. Mark the 1-inch point, like this

Draw a line, like this

and cut till you reach the fold.

Bend the two cut strips so they face in opposite directions.

Now slip the paper clip over the closed fold.

Hold the helicopter over your head. Let it go. Watch it spin — just like the rotors on a real helicopter!

Fly a Jet Plane

Jet action powers rockets, missiles, and many airplanes. Here's how to make a simple jet plane.

You will need: a drinking straw, a long piece of thin string, a balloon, a twist tie from a plastic bag, tape.

Slide the straw onto the string. Tie one end of the string to a post or tree. Stretch the string. Make sure it does not touch anything. Tie the other end to another post or tree.

Blow up the balloon. Twist the neck a few times. Seal it shut with a twist tie.

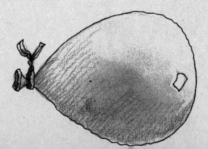

Tape the balloon to the straw. (If the string goes up and down, make sure the neck of the balloon is facing down.)

Now open the tie and untwist the balloon. See your jet plane zip away as jet action sends it forward! How far did it go?

Date: _____

Distance: _____ feet_____ inches

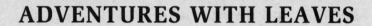

ADVENTURES WITH LEAVES

Make a Bouquet of Leaves

Most people make bouquets of flowers. But you can make a bouquet of leaves. And you can fix the bouquet so that it will last for a long time.

You will need: some branches with pretty leaves, a small bottle of glycerine from the drugstore, a vase.

Pour a mixture of half water and half glycerine into a vase. Arrange the leafy branches in the vase.

In a few days, some of the water will move up the twigs to the leaves. You may see some glycerine oozing out on the leaves. Wipe it off. What remains will make the leaves look fresh and natural for a long while.

Make a Leaf Outline

You will need: a leaf, paint, a soft brush, a piece of paper.

Find a leaf that is not torn or broken. Lay the leaf flat on a piece of paper. Get some paint of any color and a soft paintbrush. Paint from the center of the leaf out onto the paper.

When you have finished, carefully take away the leaf. You will find the perfect outline of the leaf on the paper.

Here are some leaf shapes.

Aspen

Beech

Birch

Oak

Maple

Willow

Which tree did your leaf come from? Write the name of the tree on the paper.

When you have a few leaf outlines, put them together into a book.

Make a Leaf Pressing

You will need: leaves, paper towels, a heavy weight, paste, pieces of paper.

Find a few different kinds of leaves. Put each leaf between two paper towels. Make a pile of the leaves and paper towels.

Set the pile on a flat table. Put a heavy weight on top of the pile. Use a thick book, such as a dictionary, or some bricks.

Maple

Aspen

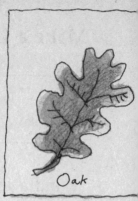

Oak

Leave the weight there for about two weeks. At the end of that time, remove the pressed leaves. Paste the leaves on pieces of paper. On each paper, write the name of the tree the leaves came from.

Put the sheets of paper together into a book.

Make a Bark Rubbing

You will need: a crayon with the paper removed, several pieces of paper.

Each kind of tree has its own special leaves. Each kind of tree also has its own special bark. You can see this if you make a rubbing of the bark of different trees.

To make a bark rubbing, hold a piece of paper tightly against the tree trunk. Rub the side of the crayon lightly over the entire paper. The paper will show an exact picture of that tree's bark. Write the name of the tree on the paper.

When you have several bark rubbings, put them all together into a book.

SNOWY DAY ADVENTURES

Make Some Snow Ice Cream

> You will need: a big bowl, sugar, cocoa, chocolate syrup, or vanilla extract, milk.

Collect a bowl of clean, fresh snow. Bring it into the house.

Sprinkle some sugar on top. Add some cocoa, chocolate syrup, or vanilla extract. Pour in a little milk. Stir with a spoon to make it slushy.

Eat your snow ice cream with the spoon. Or you can sip it through a straw.

Make a Snow Gauge

Weather reports tell how many inches of snow have fallen. But you don't need to wait for the report. You can make a simple tool to measure snowfall up to 1 foot deep.

> You will need: a clean, empty coffee can, a ruler.

As soon as it starts to snow, set out the can. Put it far from trees or houses. Surround the can with stones or earth to keep it from blowing over. Set the ruler inside the can with the 1-inch mark on the bottom.

When the snow stops, check the can and ruler. How many inches of snow are in your snow gauge? Compare your figure with the weather report.

Track the Animals

When animals walk on snow, they leave tracks. You can learn to match the tracks to the animal.

Look at the chart below of some common animal tracks.

Dog   Cat   Rabbit

Which ones have you seen? When? Where?

Animal Tracks   When Seen   Where Seen

_____

_____

_____

_____

_____

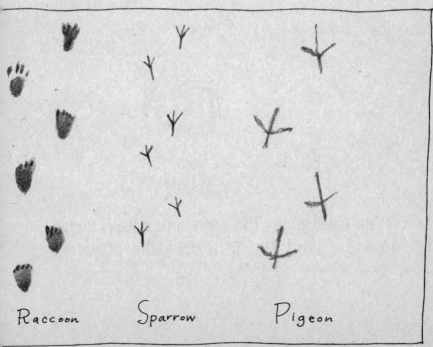

Raccoon   Sparrow   Pigeon

HANDS-IN-THE-SAND ADVENTURES

Secrets in the Sand

Sand — on a beach, river bank, dune, or field — holds many secrets. Most grains of sand are tiny bits broken off from rocks. They are broken off by
- ocean waves.
- flowing rivers.
- falling rain.

You can unlock the secrets this way: Pick up some sand. Put it in the palm of your hand. Look closely at the color of the grains of sand. The color tells you what kind of rock it comes from.

Do you see yellow grains? Yellow grains are usually quartz. Quartz is a very hard stone. It is used to make sandpaper.

Do you see gray grains? Gray grains usually come from granite. Granite is a very strong stone. Many tall buildings are made of granite.

Do you see pink grains? Pink grains are usually feldspar. Lots of rocks contain feldspar. Grains of feldspar easily break off these rocks.

Do you see red grains? Red grains may be garnet. The most beautiful garnets are used in jewelry. Some workers use garnets to cut and polish other gems.

Do you see white grains? Most white grains don't come from rocks at all. They come from the shells of clams, oysters, and other sea creatures. The water and other animals smash the shells and turn them into grains of white sand.

Do you see black grains? Many black grains are lava. Lava comes from volcanoes. It forms a black rock around the volcano. Tiny bits of lava break off. They become grains of black sand.

Sand Color   **Rock Source**

_____

_____

_____

_____

_____

_____

Look for Iron in Sand

Most sand comes from rocks. But some grains of sand are metal. Here's how to find grains of iron in the sand.

> You will need: a magnet.

Take the magnet to the beach. Slowly move it around on the sand.

Do any grains of sand stick to the magnet? They are grains of iron. You'll see that most grains of iron are black in color.

Make a Sand Casting

Many objects you find in the sand can be kept forever in a sand cast.

You will need: a box of plaster of Paris powder, an old pie tin.

Collect some small, pretty pebbles and shells. Dig a hole with sloping sides in the sand. Place the shells and pebbles on the sides of the hole.

Mix with old spoon

Plaster of Paris

hole with sloped sides

shells & pebbles

Pour the plaster of Paris powder into the pie tin. Slowly add water — either water you brought from home or water from the ocean, river, or lake. Mix the powder and water until the mixture is as thick as honey.

Pour the plaster into the hole. Let it harden.

After about a half hour, carefully dig up your sand casting. Your treasures will be set in the solid plaster.

Wrap the casting in an old newspaper. Take it home.

Let the casting harden for a few more hours. Then wash away the sand that stuck to the casting. You can keep the casting or give it to someone as a gift.

IT'S ABOUT TIME

Suppose you are outdoors without a watch. Can you tell the time? Of course you can!

Become a Sundial

A sundial uses the shadow cast by the moving sun to tell the approximate time of day. You can make a simple sundial using your own body to cast the shadow.

On a sunny day, use a compass or landmark to find north. Face that way.

Stick your left arm straight out to the side. Does the shadow of your body fall right under your arm? Then it's 6 o'clock in the morning or 6 A.M.

6am

Does your shadow fall a little more to the front instead of to your side? That's 7 A.M. A little more to the front? That's 8 A.M.

Does your shadow fall halfway between your side and straight in front of you? That's 9 A.M.

Does your shadow fall more to the front? That's 10 A.M. or 11 A.M.

Is your shadow straight ahead of you? Or is there no shadow at all? Then it's 12 noon.

Does your shadow fall a little toward your right side? That's 1 o'clock in the afternoon or 1 P.M. A little more to the side is 2 P.M.

Does your shadow fall halfway between straight in front and your side? That's 3 P.M.

As your shadow moves to the right side, you pass 4 P.M. and 5 P.M.

If your shadow falls straight out to the right side, it's 6 P.M.

Here's the date and time I used myself as a sundial:

Date: _____ Time: _____

Telling Time at Night

Your sundial works very well on sunny days. But how can you tell time at night without a watch? Here's one way.

Face north on a clear night. Find the Big Dipper and the North Star. (See pages 3 and 6.) The North Star is the last star in the handle of another group of stars that looks like the Big Dipper. But this group is smaller than the Big Dipper. It's called the Little Dipper.

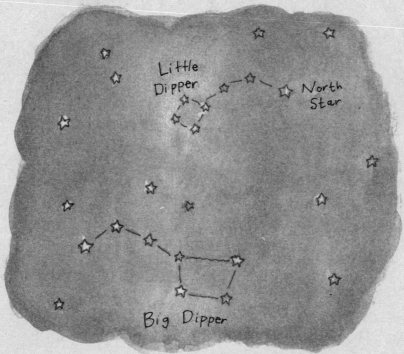

Every night the Little Dipper seems to swing around the North Star. Sometimes the cup points down. Sometimes it points to a side. Sometimes it points up.

This chart shows how the Little Dipper turns. It shows the positions for 6 P.M., midnight, and 6 A.M. The Little Dipper slowly turns from 6 P.M. to midnight to 6 A.M.

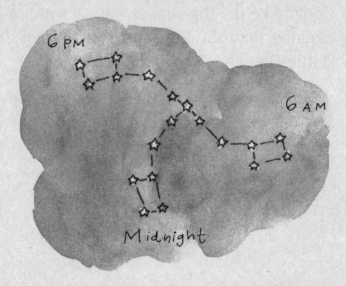

If the Little Dipper is halfway between 6 P.M. and midnight, it's 9 P.M. If the Little Dipper is halfway between midnight and 6 A.M., it's 3 A.M.

Here's the date, the time, and a picture of the Little Dipper that I saw.

Date: _____

Time: _____

THIS IS FOR THE BIRDS

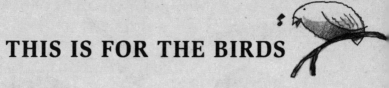

Make a Pinecone Bird Feeder

Birds need to eat a lot in winter to stay warm. You can help by giving them food in homemade feeders.

> You will need: a jar of peanut butter, a plastic knife, a length of string, a large pinecone.

Tie the string to the top of the pinecone. Use the plastic knife to smear peanut butter all over the cone.

Now find a place to hang your pinecone feeder. Hang it from
— a tree branch.
— a part of your house.
— a fence.
— a pole.

Try to find a place that is near trees or bushes. Those are places the birds can hide if there is danger.

Also, try to find a spot near your kitchen window. Birds mostly feed in the morning. You might be able to watch them feed while you eat your breakfast.

Keep a log of the birds that come to your feeder. (See Keep a Bird Log on page 48.)

Make a Milk Carton Bird Feeder

Another kind of bird feeder can be made from a milk carton.

> You will need: an empty half-gallon milk carton, tape, scissors, string, birdseed.

Wash and dry the milk carton. Use the tape to close the opening on top.

With a grown-up's help, cut out two opposite sides of the carton, leaving about 2 inches on the bottom and 1 inch on the sides and top. Then ask the grown-up to make two small, far-apart holes in the top of the carton.

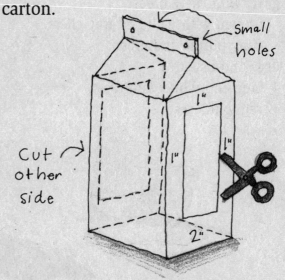

Small holes

Cut other side

1"

1"

1"

2"

Thread the string through the two small holes. You will use this string to hang up your bird feeder.

Fill the bottom of the carton with birdseed. Hang up the filled bird feeder. (See page 45 for places to hang the feeder.) Add more birdseed as needed.

Keep a Bird Log

Bird feeders attract many different kinds of birds. It's fun to keep a log of the various species that come to your feeder.

Here's a list of some common birds. It tells what each one looks like.

Robin — gray, with rusty breast.
Sparrow — brown, with white or gray chest.
Starling — shiny purple and green.
Crow — large and black.
Blue jay — blue and white with crest.
Cardinal — red with crest.

Robin

Sparrow

Starling

Cardinal

Blue Jay

Crow

Fill in the log:

Bird	Date Seen	Hour

Build a Milk Carton Birdhouse

Some birds roost or build their nests in birdhouses. It's easy to help the birds by turning a milk carton into a birdhouse.

> You will need: an empty half-gallon milk carton, tape, scissors, string.

Wash and dry the milk carton. Use the tape to close the top opening to the carton.

With a grown-up's help, cut a round entrance hole near the top of the carton for the birds to enter. How big should you make the hole? It depends on the bird species you want to attract. See the chart below.

Bird	Entrance Hole
Bluebird	1 ½ inches across
Chickadee	1 ⅛ inches across
Titmouse	1 ¼ inches across
Downy woodpecker	1 ¼ inches across
House wren	1 inch across

Also, ask the adult to poke two far-apart small holes in the top of the carton. Thread the string through the two holes. You will use this string to hang up your birdhouse.

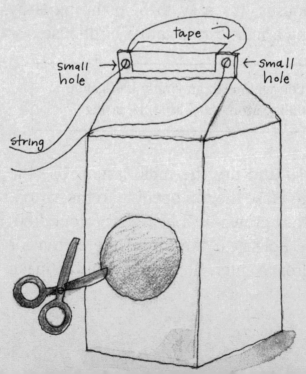

Collect some grass cuttings and toss them inside the birdhouse.

Ask a grown-up to help you hang your birdhouse from a tree or pole. It should be about 8 feet above the ground. Set it up early in the spring, before the birds return. Then wait for a bird to come and make itself at home.

BE A ROCK HOUND

Find Bedrock

The solid part of Earth is called the bedrock. Earth's soil lies on the bedrock — just as you lie on your bed. You find bedrock under all the land and under all the water.

In some places the bedrock is at the surface. In other places it is far beneath the surface.

Look in a park. Look on a rocky hill. See if you can find a big, solid rock sticking up out of the ground. That's bedrock at the surface.

Can you find some small stones around the bedrock? Do they look the same as the bedrock?

They are stones that broke off from the bedrock. Feel the edges. They are sharp.

Save a small stone from the bedrock. Put it in a plastic sandwich bag. On a piece of paper, write where you got the stone. Put the paper in with the stone.

Every place you go, look for different kinds of bedrock. Find bedrock of different colors. Find smoother or rougher kinds of bedrock.

Pick up a small stone from around each kind of bedrock. Soon you will have a good collection.

Smooth Stones

The stones that break off from bedrock have sharp edges. Yet many stones you see are smooth. Can you guess why?

Long ago, the rough stones fell into either a river or an ocean. They were carried long distances by the water or the waves. They kept bumping into other stones. The sharp edges kept wearing down. Soon the stones were smooth and round.

Find a stone that is smooth and round. Add it to your collection.

Find a stone that is smooth and flat. Add that one to your collection, too.

Collect Colored Stones

Stones come in many different colors — red, white, black, yellow, gray, and so on. Some are mixtures of a few colors.

Stones get their colors from the minerals they contain. A mineral is something that is dug from the earth. It is not alive.

Some stones contain only one mineral. They are one color. Some stones contain more than one mineral. They are a mixture of colors.

It's fun to make a collection of stones of different colors.

You will need: an empty egg carton.

Look around for small, different colored stones. Put each stone in a separate cup in the egg carton.

Get a book that tells about rocks or minerals. Match your stones to the pictures in the book. Write each name on a piece of paper. Put the paper in with the stone.

Here's a list of the stones in my collection:

_____ _____

_____ _____

_____ _____

BLOWING WINDS

Measuring the Speed of the Wind

The National Weather Service has instruments that measure exact wind speed. But you can estimate how strong the wind is blowing just by looking around you.

A British admiral, Sir Francis Beaufort, figured out a way to do this. It is called the Beaufort Scale.

Signs of Wind	Type of Wind	MPH*
Smoke goes straight up	Calm	0
Smoke drifts	Light air	1–3
Leaves rustle	Light breeze	4–7
Leaves move	Gentle breeze	8–12
Branches move	Moderate breeze	13–18
Small trees sway	Fresh breeze	19–24
Big branches move	Strong breeze	25–31
Big trees sway	Moderate gale	32–38
Twigs break off	Fresh gale	39–46
Signs and antennas blow	Strong gale	47–54
Big trees fall	Whole gale	55–63
Much damage	Storm	64–74
Terrible damage	Hurricane	75 +

*Miles per hour

Look for signs, such as smoke rising or leaves moving. Then check the Beaufort Scale. Enter the date, wind type, and wind speed in the log below.

Date	Wind Type	Speed

Make Wind Chimes

You can use the wind to make music with wind chimes.

You will need: five large nails or old keys that no one needs, 5 feet of string, a ruler, scissors.

Cut five lengths of string, each 1 foot long. Tie a nail or key to the end of each string.

Find a place close to your house to hang the wind chimes. A tree limb or a railing are good places. Tie the strings so that the nails or keys are very close to each other —but not touching.

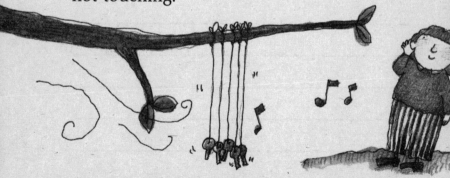

Now wait for a breeze to make beautiful music.

LISTEN HERE!

Three-Way String Telephone

Sound waves pass through the air. But sound waves can also pass through solids — like string. You can send sound waves through string with a string telephone and have a three-way phone call.

You will need: three empty, clean cottage cheese or margarine containers without covers, two lengths of thin string each 6–10 feet long, a nail.

Use the nail to poke a hole in the bottom of each container. Push one end of one string through the hole in one container. Tie a big knot.

Push the other end of that string through the hole in another container. Tie another big knot. Pull the string so the knots rest on the bottoms of the containers.

Wrap the end of the other length of string around the middle of the string connecting the two containers. Tie a knot there. Push the other end of the second string through the bottom of the third container. Tie a big knot.

Give two of the containers to friends. Ask them to walk away with the containers until both lengths of string are tight. Tell them to hold the container to the ear without touching the string.

Now speak softly into the open end of your container. Your friends will hear you clearly.

The container picks up the sound waves of your voice. It sends them into the string. The string carries the sound waves to your friends' ears. The other containers let your friends hear your voice.

Now switch. You hold the container to your ear. Let one friend and then the other speak softly into their containers. You'll hear each other clearly.

Garden Hose Telephone

Sound waves pass through air. They pass through solids. But did you know that they also pass through tubes? Sometimes tubes carry sound waves best of all. Try it out.

You will need: a garden hose (emptied of all water), two funnels.

Stick the narrow part of one funnel into one end of the hose. Then put the second funnel into the other end.

One person talks into the funnel at a time. Take turns talking and listening.

Seeing by Sound

You see with your eyes. You hear with your ears. But do you know you can "see" with your ears? Lots of animals do!

Bats mostly fly at night when it is hard to see. Whales swim in the water where it is hard to see. Lots of other animals can't use their eyes. How do they avoid bumping into things?

As they move about, animals make sounds. They listen for how long it takes for the sound to bounce back. If it takes a long time, they're safe. Nothing is close by. If it takes a short time, they have to watch out. Something is close by.

Since the animals listen for the echo — and since the echo helps them find their location — seeing by sound is called *echolocation*.

You can try out echolocation. Stand about 6 feet away from a big wall. Face the wall. Close your eyes.

Clap your hands together once very hard. Carefully listen to the sound.

Now take two big steps forward. Clap your hands again. Listen. Do you hear any difference in the sound?

Clapping your hands, slowly walk toward the wall. Then slowly walk away from the wall clapping your hands. Notice the difference.

Many blind people tap a cane on the street as they walk. Partly, they are feeling for anything in their way. Partly, they are listening to the sound and using echolocation to guide them. You can try this way of using echolocation.

> You will need: a cane or yardstick and a friend to help.

Take the cane or yardstick to a paved street. Close your eyes and tap the cane on the ground as you walk. Use the echo of the sounds to guide you. Ask your friend to go along to make sure you avoid danger.

Describe your experience: _____

_____

_____

Tap

BUGS AT WORK

Buried Treasure

Most garbage gets buried. But what happens to garbage after that? Here's how you can find out.

> You will need: an old piece of bread, an apple core or a piece of spoiled fruit, a lettuce leaf or vegetable leftover, a small glass jar, a plastic cup, bottle, or old toy.

Find a place where you can dig five small holes. Dig the holes about 5 inches deep. Bury each item. Pour some water in each

hole. Fill the holes with soil. Mark the five holes.

Wait at least a month. Wait longer if you made the holes in sand or during the cold weather.

Now, dig up the five items. What did you find?

_____

The glass and plastic did not change at all. But what about the bread, fruit, and vegetable? What happened to them?_____

_____

Germs, bugs, and worms in the soil ate them. They changed them into more soil.

It takes about a month for foods to become part of the soil. It takes paper a year or so to become part of the soil. It takes metals hundreds of years to become part of the soil. But most glass and plastic *never* become part of the soil!

Back to the Earth

Each of us throws away about 3 pounds of food garbage every day! We also throw away grass clippings in the summer and dead leaves in the fall.

Did you know that you can use most of what you throw away to make good, rich soil? This special soil is called compost. Here's how to make your own compost.

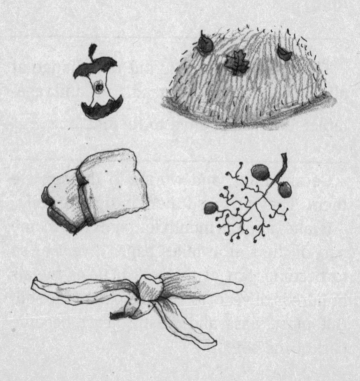

Find a corner of your yard or a nearby vacant lot where nothing is growing. Every day throw all your food wastes there. Don't add any meat or dairy foods, though. They make the compost smelly. Also add yard wastes to the compost pile.

Every once in a while
— sprinkle some water on the compost.
— throw some soil on the pile.
— use a shovel to turn over the compost.

In about a month the garbage will turn into dark brown compost. Add the compost to ordinary garden soil. Or mix it with soil in a flowerpot before planting. Compost helps plants grow.

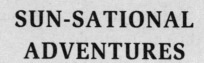

SUN-SATIONAL ADVENTURES

Cooking by Sunlight

More and more people use the heat energy from the sun to warm their houses. They also use the sun's energy to make hot water. But did you know you can cook food with heat energy from the sun?

> You will need: a large mixing bowl, aluminum foil, a hot dog or marshmallow.

Cover the entire inside of the bowl with aluminum foil. Make sure that the aluminum foil is shiny-side up.

On a hot, sunny day set your sunlight cooker in the bright sunlight. Be sure the cooker gets the direct rays of the sun. Move your hand around inside the bowl until you find the very hottest spot.

Now put the hot dog or marshmallow at

the end of a long stick or fork. Hold it at the hottest spot in the bowl while it cooks. In a while the hot dog will be steamy hot or the marshmallow will start to melt. Eat and enjoy!

Tracking the Sun

You know that the planet Earth is always spinning around. To people on Earth, it looks as though the sun is moving across the sky. Here's a way to follow the path of the sun across the sky.

> You will need: a magnifying glass, tape, a piece of paper.

Find a sunny place away from trees or buildings. Move the magnifying glass up and down until you see it make a bright spot on the ground.

Find a chair, post, or fence that is about the same height. Tape the magnifying glass over the edge.

Set a clean piece of white paper on the ground under the magnifying glass. Hold it in place with small stones around the edge.

Draw a circle around the bright spot on the paper. Leave the magnifying glass and paper in place for about an hour.

Sun's rays

Look at the paper again. Is the spot still in the same place? No. It has moved. As the sun moved in the sky, the spot moved. Draw a circle around the new spot.

Keep checking every hour. And every hour draw a new circle. When you are done, the circles will show you the track of the sun across the sky.

Copy the track of the sun here:

SEEING AROUND CORNERS

Make a Periscope

> You will need: a long pole or old broom handle, a thumbtack, a large paper clip, a small mirror.

A periscope lets you see around corners, behind you, and above your head. Most periscopes have two mirrors to let you see in different directions. Here's how to make a simple periscope with just one mirror.

Attach the paper clip to the end of the pole with the thumbtack. Put the thumbtack through the part of the paper clip that has a single loop. You may have to use a hammer if the wood is very hard.

Next, bend the double-loop part of the paper clip halfway up. Hold the thumbtack down while you bend the paper clip.

Slip the mirror into the paper clip. Now you're ready to use your periscope.

Stand at the corner of a building. Hold out
your periscope. What do you see on the
other side of the building?

_____

Look for a bird's nest in a tree. Hold up
your periscope. What do you see inside the

nest? _____

CREEPY CRAWLERS

The World of Worms

Worms are great workers. They
— break up clumps of soil.
— allow air into the soil.
— eat decaying matter and turn it into soil.
Here's how to watch some worms at work.

You will need: a large, clean glass bottle with a wide cover, a small nail, soil, a flashlight.

Use the nail to punch some holes in the cover. Put some soil in the bottle. Try to find soils of different colors:
— dark brown soil.
— light tan soil.
— yellow sand.
— black potting soil.
Press down the layers of soil. Leave about 2 inches of space above the top of the soil.

Use a flashlight to look for worms in the evening after a rain shower. Worms are more active in the dark. And they come to the surface when the ground is wet.

Be sure to step lightly as you walk. Worms can feel the vibrations of footsteps. They will hide in their tunnels if they sense you coming.

Put the worms you catch into your bottle. Sprinkle enough water on the soil to make it moist. Also, add a few dead leaves to feed the worms.

Cover the bottle and set it outside in a safe place. Cover it with a heavy old towel to make it dark. From time to time, add more water and leaves.

Every day look at the worms. Check what you see.

Are the worms

    — crawling around? _____

    — mixing soil from one layer to an-

      other? _____

    — eating the leaves? _____

    — making tunnels in the earth? _____

After a week, set the worms free. Just dump the soil and worms on the ground. Watch them crawl away.

Give Me Air

The ground under your feet feels solid. But there is lots of air hidden in with the soil.

When it rains, the water soaks into the soil. It forces out the air.

Worms need the air to breathe. That's why they come up out of the soil after it rains.

You will need: a clean, empty glass jar.

Catch some worms after a rain. Put them in the bottom of the jar. Pile soil on top of them. (Don't worry. This won't hurt the worms.) Then pour lots of water on top of the soil.

Do the worms crawl up to the surface?

After you finish this activity, set the worms free.

Make a Spiderweb Picture

Spiders spin webs to catch insects. The insects get trapped in the sticky web. Then the spiders kill and eat the insects.

A spiderweb is made of thin silk thread that comes from a spider's body. It forms a beautiful design. You can save the spiderweb design.

You will need: some flour or talcum powder, a big piece of cardboard, hair spray.

Find a pretty spiderweb (without a spider). Sprinkle some flour or powder on the palm of your hand. Gently blow it over the web. The flour or powder makes it easy to see the silk threads.

Spray a thin layer of hair spray on the cardboard. Hold the cardboard behind and at the same angle as the web. Slowly and carefully move the cardboard forward. Catch the web on the cardboard. Spray it again with a thin layer of hair spray.

Study the spiderweb. Can you see how the spider spun the web? What was its starting point?

GARDENS BIG AND SMALL

Growing plants can be lots of fun. Just remember what plants need to grow: sun, water, air, food, and soil.

Start a Flower Garden

Find a sunny outdoor spot to start a garden. Make it at least 3 feet long by 3 feet wide.

> You will need: a shovel, a rake, fertilizer, flower seeds.

Loosen the soil. Spread about a bag of fertilizer on the ground. Use your shovel to mix the fertilizer in with the soil. Smooth the ground with your rake.

Buy three packets of flower seeds. Marigolds, nasturtiums, and zinnias are easy to grow.

Poke a row of little holes about 1 foot apart. Drop three seeds into each hole.

Water. Cover with soil. Pat with your hand and water lightly. Use markers to show where you planted each kind of seed.

After a few weeks your seeds will grow stems. Water every three days. Watch them grow leaves and then flowers.

Grow Tomato Plants

Suppose you have no room for a garden. Then you can grow plants outdoors in a container.

You will need: tomato seeds, a ruler, plant food, several half-gallon milk containers, garden or potting soil.

Cut off the top of a milk container and fill it with soil. Poke six small holes in the soil with your finger. Put tomato seeds in each one. Water gently. Cover the holes with a layer of soil. Put the container in a sunny spot.

Check the soil every day. Add enough water to keep the soil damp. After about two weeks, tiny green seedlings will pop up.

Measure the heights of the seedlings. When they are about 4 inches high, they are ready to be moved.

Place layers of soil in the other containers. Take the biggest seedlings. Carefully dig them up.

Gently place each seedling in its own container. Add soil up to the level of the lower leaves. Water the plants. Add plant food to the containers every three weeks. Keep them outdoors in a sunny spot.

In a month or two, the plants will be quite tall. Set tall sticks or stakes in the soil and fasten the growing plants to them with twist ties.

After about three months, look for flowers and then for small, green tomatoes to appear. Slowly the tomatoes will grow bigger and redder. When they come off the vine easily, it's picking time.

WEATHER WISDOM

What Will the Weather Be?

Do you want to know what the weather will be tomorrow? Farmers and sailors have found ways to forecast the weather. Try their methods. See if they really work.

Is the sunset bright and red? That means it is likely to be clear and sunny tomorrow.

Is there a ring around the moon? That means it is likely to be rainy or stormy tomorrow.

Is the night sky clear and the wind light? That means it is likely to be cooler tomorrow.

Is it cloudy tonight? That means it is likely to be warmer tomorrow.

Date	Weather Today	Weather Forecast

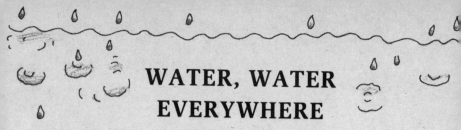

WATER, WATER EVERYWHERE

Rain on the Ground

Go out after a heavy rain. Look at a lawn or field. What do you see?

It may look muddy. But you see very little water. Do you know why?

The rainwater soaked down through the soil. As the water moved down, the soil took out most of the dirt in the water. The water got cleaner and cleaner.

Finally the water hit a layer of rock. It could sink no lower. The water became part of a pool of water under the ground. Such a body of water is called an *aquifer*.

People dig wells to get the water up from an aquifer. And the water that comes up is usually clean and fresh.

You can make your own aquifer.

> You will need: a large plastic cup, soil, pebbles, water.

Muddy Water

Soil

Pebbles

Place a layer of pebbles in the cup. Place a layer of soil on top.

Mix a little soil with the water to make the water muddy. Pour the muddy water into the cup.

Watch the water soak through the soil and pebbles in the cup. The bottom of the cup is like the rock under the ground. It stops the water. The water forms into a pool.

It is like a tiny aquifer.

Look closely at the water at the bottom of the cup. Is it clearer than the muddy water you poured in? The soil and pebbles cleaned the water.

Water From Leaves

The roots of all plants take in water from the soil. Some of this water moves up to the leaves of the plant. And the leaves give off some of this water. You can see that leaves give off water with this activity.

You will need: a tree twig with leaves or a small plant, a dry plastic bag, tape or twist tie or string.

Slip the plastic bag over the leaves. Shut the opening of the bag with the tape, twist tie, or string.

Leave the plastic bag in place for a few days. Then look at the bag. You'll see drops of water inside the bag. The water came from the leaves inside the bag. After you've seen the drops of water, take the bag off.

Write your conclusion here:

_____

_____

Water in Your Breath

Nearly 70 percent of your body is water. Every time you breathe out, some water comes out as water vapor.

You can see this on the next cold day. Open your mouth very wide. Breathe out. Do you see a tiny cloud form in front of your mouth? That is caused by the water vapor in your breath.

The water vapor in your breath is warm. When it hits the cold air, the water vapor turns into water. The cloud you see is made up of tiny drops of water. The change from water vapor into drops of water is called *condensation*.

You can also see condensation in warmer weather.

You will need: a mirror or a pair of eye-glasses or sunglasses.

Open your mouth as wide as you can. Hold the mirror or glasses just inside your mouth. Breathe out.

You'll see a damp spot on the mirror or glasses. Can you tell why? The mirror or glasses are colder than your breath. The water vapor in your breath condenses on the glass.

A WALK IN TOWN

Watch Your Step!

Most streets and sidewalks in towns and cities are paved. Take a walk in town and discover the materials that are used for paving.

Is the paving solid black? Then it is probably asphalt. Asphalt is made from oil. Road builders first heat the asphalt. Then they pour the warm asphalt on the street and use a heavy roller to make it smooth. When the asphalt cools, it becomes a solid. Asphalt is sometimes called blacktop.

Is the paving black with many small stones or gravel mixed in? Then it is probably macadam (muh-KAD-um). To make macadam, the road builders mix small stones or gravel with asphalt. Then they pour the mixture, smooth it down, and let it cool and become solid.

Is the paving gray? Then it is probably concrete. Road builders mix cement powder, sand, gravel, and water to make concrete. They pour the concrete mixture, smooth it down, and let it stand until it becomes hard.

Notice the lines cut in the concrete streets or sidewalks. They are there to protect the concrete.

When it gets hot, concrete spreads out. It expands. The lines in the concrete give it room to expand. Without the lines, the concrete would crack and break in hot weather.

Write down the places where you found asphalt, macadam, and concrete paving.

Where?	Street or Sidewalk?
Asphalt _____	
Macadam _____	
Concrete _____	

What's on the Outside of Buildings?

On a walk in town, you may pass many different kinds of buildings. What material covers the outside of these buildings?

Is it wood? Many one-family homes are covered with wood. The usual woods used for this are pine, fir, or cedar.

Is it brick? Many small and large buildings are covered with brick. Bricks are made from clay and water. To make the bricks, the clay and water are heated as high as 2000° F. Bricks are strong, fireproof, and waterproof.

Is it aluminum? Aluminum is a metal that is sometimes put on top of other surfaces, such as wood or brick. The aluminum is attached to buildings in long, side-to-side strips. It is usually painted a bright color.

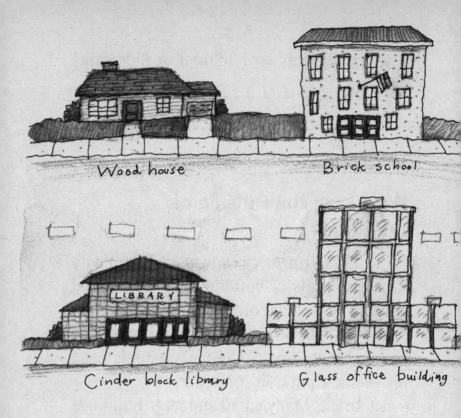

Wood house

Brick school

Cinder block library

Glass office building

Sometimes it looks like wood. But if you tap it, you can hear that it is metal.

Is it glass? Most buildings have some glass on the outside. Most houses and stores have glass windows. Many stores have glass doors. Glass is made by melting a mixture of sand and other chemicals.

Is it cinder block? Cinder blocks are large gray blocks made of cement. They are partly hollow, so they are light to carry. Yet they are very strong. They are usually painted a bright color.

Is it marble? Marble was formed from the bodies of sea animals that died millions of years ago. It is used on some public buildings and banks. Marble comes in many different colors and is very beautiful.

Is it granite? Granite is a strong gray stone. You'll find it on many libraries, schools, and public buildings. If you look closely, you'll see shiny or colored specks in the granite.

Try to find one building of each kind of material. Which building?

Wood _____

Brick _____

Aluminum _____

Glass _____

Cinder block _____

Marble _____

Granite _____

My house is covered with _____

A WALK IN THE COUNTRY

See the Tree

You can't walk far in the country without seeing a tree.

More than 1,000 different kinds of trees grow in the United States. They can be divided into two kinds. One kind has thin needle leaves. Pine, spruce, fir, and hemlock have needle leaves.

Trees with needle leaves are called evergreens. Their needle leaves stay green all year long. They don't fall off the trees. Take a walk in the country.

Do you see any needle-leaf trees?
Yes __ No __

The other kind of tree has broad leaves. Oak, maple, elm, and chestnut have broad leaves. Every fall their leaves change color and fall off. New leaves start to grow in the spring.

Do you see any broad-leaf trees?
Yes __ No __

Oak

Fir

Maple

Elm

The leaves on broad-leaf trees are green during the spring and summer. In the fall the tree stops making the chemical that colors the leaves green. The leaves turn red or yellow.

Later in the fall the leaves die. They turn brown and fall off the trees.

You can tell one broad-leaf tree from another by the shape of its leaves. Which ones did you see on your walk? (See the chart of leaf shapes on page 26.)

Make a list of the trees you have seen.

_____   _____

_____   _____

_____   _____

Plants on Parade

You'll see trees on a walk in the country. You'll also see bushes. Bushes are smaller than trees. They do not have big trunks like trees. But they do have wooden branches.

On trees, bushes, or on the ground, you'll see a colorful display. These are the flowers. The seeds of many plants grow in the flowers. Some of the seeds that fall to the ground begin new plants.

There are thousands of different kinds of flowers. Here are a few kinds. Check the types of flowers you see on your walk.

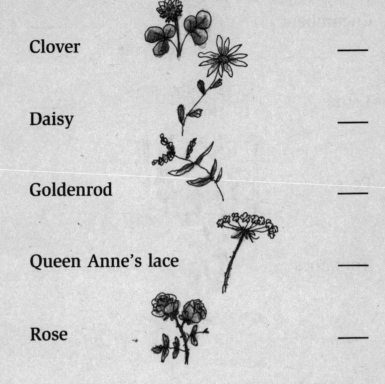

Clover   —

Daisy   —

Goldenrod   —

Queen Anne's lace   —

Rose   —

Your walk may take you past a garden or farm. Here, plants that we eat as food are grown. Check the ones you have seen.

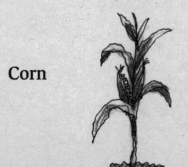

Corn   —

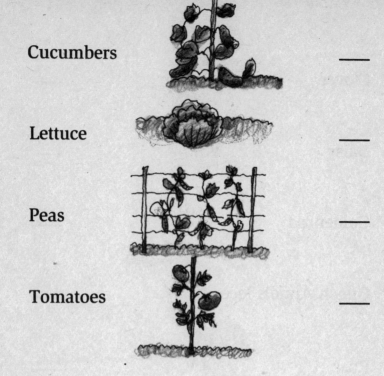

Cucumbers ___

Lettuce ___

Peas ___

Tomatoes ___

A plant that grows where it is not wanted is called a weed. Weeds also keep plants that *are* wanted from growing. Any field that is not cared for has lots and lots of weeds. Check the weeds you have seen.

Chickweed ___

Crabgrass   —

Dandelion   —

Plantain   —

Ragweed   —

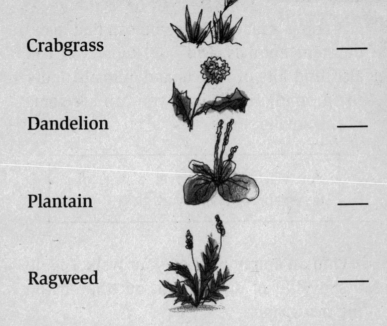

You may see another kind of plant on your walk. This plant is shaped like a small umbrella. It grows on the ground, often in shady, damp spots. But it also grows on trees and logs. It is white or brown in color.

Have you seen a plant like this?

It's a mushroom.

Zoo Under the Ground

A zoo is a place where you can find many different animals. Did you know you can also find lots of insects and animals under the ground? Here's how you can see some of the smaller ones.

> You will need: a shovel, a page of a newspaper, a magnifying glass.

Find an empty field on your walk. Dig up a shovelful of dirt. Spread out the dirt on the newspaper.

Look closely at the dirt with your magnifying glass.

Do you see any worms? ____
Do you see any ants? ____

Describe any other creatures you see:

_____

_____

_____

When you are finished, put back the earth.

Discover the "Hole" Truth

Look for holes in the ground on your walk. These holes are made by animals who live in tunnels in the ground. Chipmunks, woodchucks, skunks, and porcupines live in tunnels.

Would you like to know who lives in the holes you have seen?

> You will need: a plastic bottle of water, a small shovel.

Dig up some earth around the hole. Pour the water on the earth to make it mud.

Spread the mud around the hole. Smooth it down with the shovel.

Leave the mud overnight. The next day, see if there are any tracks in the mud. Here is what some of the tracks look like.

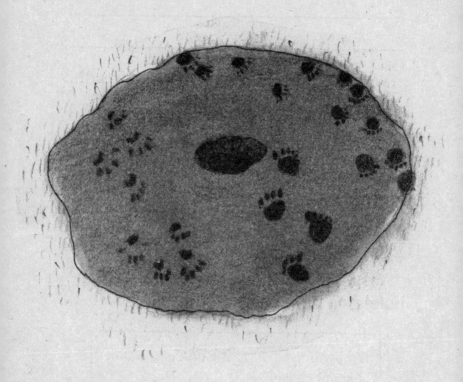

Which animal left tracks? _____

Try the same thing at different holes. See if you can discover other animal tracks.